BLACK RHINO

WRITTEN BY
E.C. ANDREWS

ENDANGERED
LIFE CYCLES

Library of Congress Control Number:
2024953105

ISBN
979-8-89359-308-2 (library bound)
979-8-89359-392-1 (paperback)
979-8-89359-367-9 (epub)
979-8-89359-338-9 (hosted ebook)

Printed in the United States of America
Mankato, MN
092025

sales@northstareditions.com
888-417-0195

Written by:
E.C. Andrews

Edited by:
Rebecca Phillips-Bartlett

Designed by:
Ker Ker Lee

All facts, statistics, web addresses and URLs in this book were verified as valid and accurate at time of writing. No responsibility for any changes to external websites or references can be accepted by either the author or publisher.

American adaptation copyright © 2026 by North Star Editions, Mendota Heights, MN 55120. All rights reserved. No part of this book may be reproduced or utilized in any form or by any means without written permission from the publisher.

Black Rhino © 2024 BookLife Publishing
This edition is published by arrangement with BookLife Publishing

Photo Credits – Images are courtesy of Shutterstock.com. With thanks to Getty Images, Thinkstock Photo and iStockphoto.

Cover – Artur Tiutenko, Icswart, Volodymyr Burdiak, VVadi4ka, MIKHAIL GRACHIKOV. Recurring – bum katya, imaginasty, VVadi4ka, Icswart, Volodymyr Burdiak. 4–5 – PCH.Vector. 6–7 – AfricaWildlife, Peter Bruins. 8–9 – Albie Venter, JULIAN LOTT. 10–11 – JMx Images, Diego Grandi. 12–13 – Lance van de Vyver, PeterScott. 14–15 – Lance van de Vyver, Maurizio Photo. 16–17 – Lance van de Vyver, Vibe Images. 18–19 – Stu Porter, Dirk M. de Boer. 20–21 – MM.Wildlifephotos, Roger de la Harpe. 22–23 – PeopleImages.com – Yuri A, Pixel-Shot.

CONTENTS

PAGE 4   What Is a Life Cycle?
PAGE 6   Black Rhinos
PAGE 8   Endangered Animals
PAGE 10 The Life Cycle Begins
PAGE 12 Being Born
PAGE 14 Newborn Calves
PAGE 16 Growing Up
PAGE 18 Adult Life
PAGE 20 Dangers
PAGE 22 The Life Cycle Continues
PAGE 24 Glossary and Index

WORDS THAT LOOK LIKE THIS CAN BE FOUND IN THE GLOSSARY ON PAGE 24.

WHAT IS A LIFE CYCLE?

All living things go through different stages. Living things include people, animals, and plants. They all change and grow over time. This change is called a life cycle.

BABY

CHILD

TEENAGER

ADULT

SENIOR

Most animals are born small. They grow as they get older. Eventually, they die. During their lives, most animals have <u>offspring</u>. This process allows the life cycle to continue.

BLACK RHINOS

Black rhinos are a type of rhinoceros. They are found in parts of Africa. They are smaller than white rhinos. Rhinos are known for their big horns.

Black rhinos are herbivores. This means they eat only plants. Black rhinos live in woodlands and grasslands. These animals can live for up to 50 years. However, they are endangered.

ENDANGERED ANIMALS

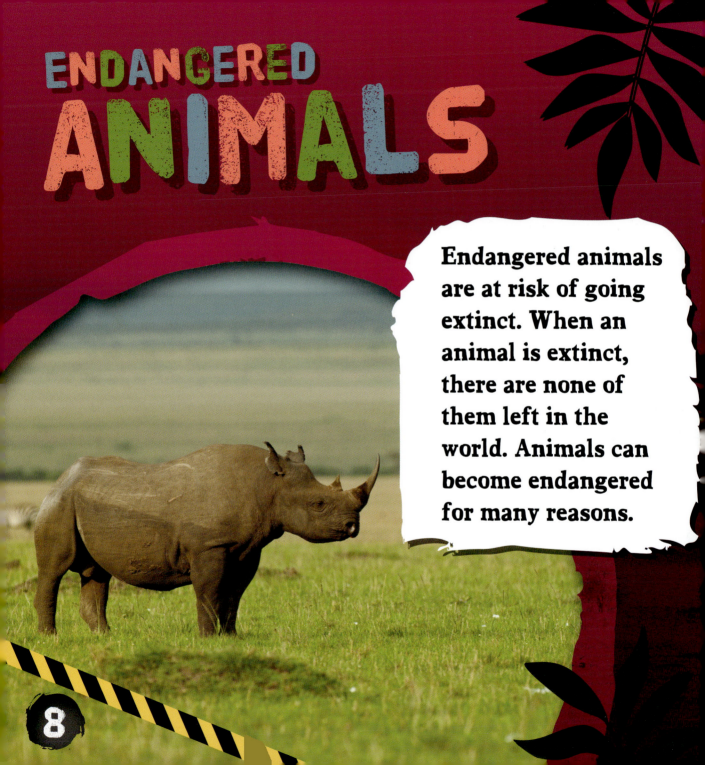

Endangered animals are at risk of going extinct. When an animal is extinct, there are none of them left in the world. Animals can become endangered for many reasons.

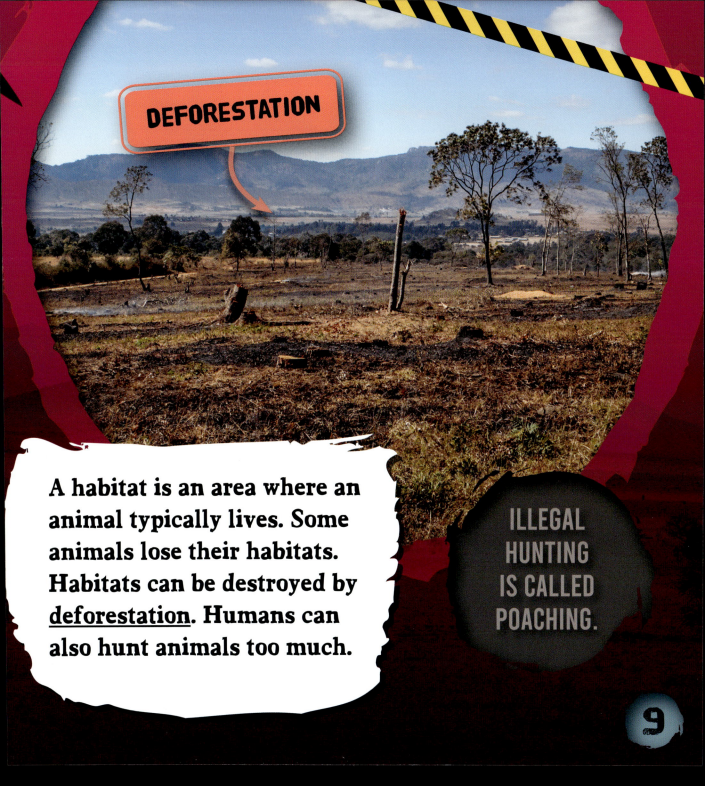

DEFORESTATION

A habitat is an area where an animal typically lives. Some animals lose their habitats. Habitats can be destroyed by <u>deforestation</u>. Humans can also hunt animals too much.

ILLEGAL HUNTING IS CALLED POACHING.

THE LIFE CYCLE BEGINS

We need to understand black rhinos' life cycles to help them. First, a rhino finds a <u>mate</u>. The male follows the female around for one to two weeks before having young together.

Baby rhinos are called calves. Female rhinos usually have calves every two to three years. The mother is pregnant for 15 to 18 months. That is about twice as long as humans!

BLACK RHINOS USUALLY HAVE ONLY ONE CALF AT A TIME.

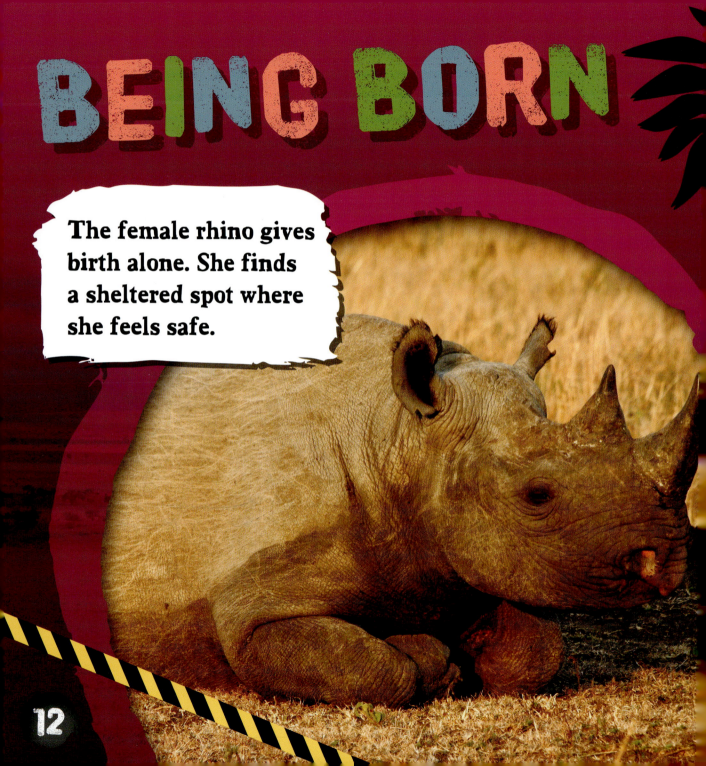

BEING BORN

The female rhino gives birth alone. She finds a sheltered spot where she feels safe.

BLACK RHINO CALF

It usually takes 30 to 45 minutes for a female rhino to give birth. The calf can stand up a few hours after it is born.

NEWBORN CALVES

Rhinos are <u>mammals</u>. Mother rhinos make milk. A newborn calf drinks its mother's milk. The calf learns how to find its own food after about one month.

The calf starts drinking water at about five months old. However, the calf keeps drinking its mother's milk until it is about one and a half years old.

GROWING UP

Calves rely on their mothers for food and protection. They have close <u>bonds</u> with their mothers. Some stay with their mothers for up to four years.

The mother teaches the calf everything it needs to know. When the mother has another calf, she sends her older calf away to live on its own.

ADULT LIFE

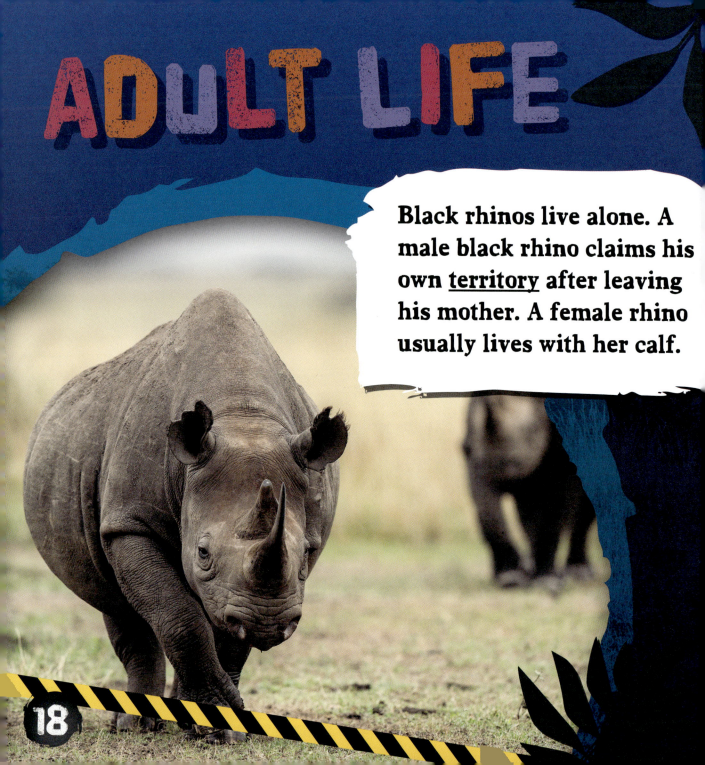

Black rhinos live alone. A male black rhino claims his own territory after leaving his mother. A female rhino usually lives with her calf.

Some black rhinos have calves of their own. This allows the life cycle to continue. Females can have calves at about four to seven years old. Males become adults between the ages of eight and ten.

DANGERS

Humans hunt black rhinos for their horns. Poachers sell rhino horns for a lot of money.

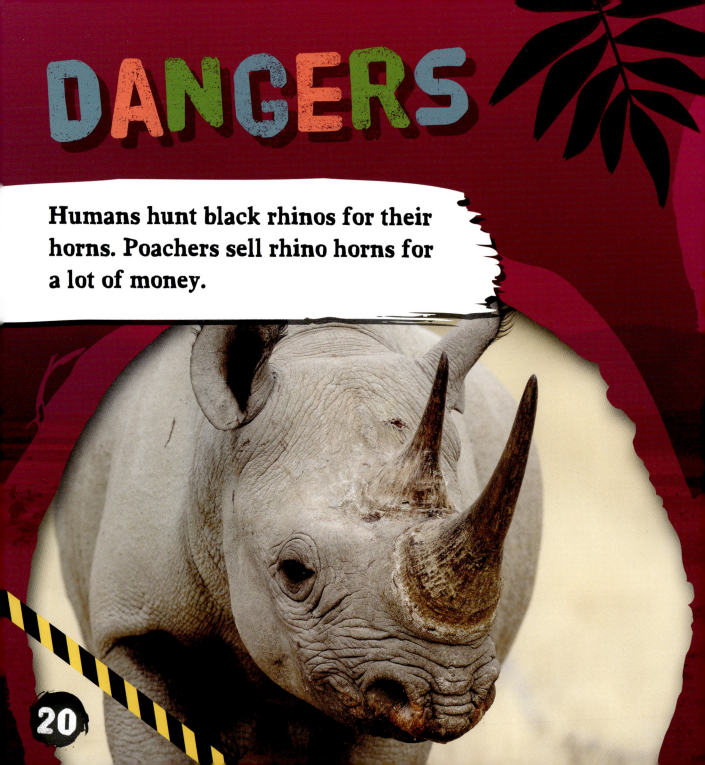

Black rhinos are also threatened by deforestation. Humans have cut down forests to build farms. Many black rhinos have lost their homes.

THE LIFE CYCLE CONTINUES

Some people work to help black rhinos. Some catch poachers. Others move black rhinos to guarded habitats where they will be safe.

A CONSERVATIONIST IS SOMEONE WHO PROTECTS ANIMALS AND THE ENVIRONMENT.

LET'S MAKE SURE THE BLACK RHINO'S LIFE CYCLE CONTINUES!

There are some small things you can do to help rhinos.

- Don't buy products made from rhino horns.
- Don't waste paper. This way, fewer trees will be cut down.

GLOSSARY

BONDS	relationships based on love, friendship, and loyalty
DEFORESTATION	the cutting down and removal of trees in a forest
ENVIRONMENT	the natural world
MAMMALS	animals that are warm-blooded, have a backbone, and produce milk to feed their young
MATE	a partner of the same species that an animal produces young with
OFFSPRING	the young of an animal, a person, or a plant
TERRITORY	an area that an animal claims and defends

INDEX

calves 11, 13–19
deforestation 9, 21
food 7, 14, 16
habitats 9, 22
horns 6, 20, 23
life cycles 4–5, 10, 19, 22–23
mates 10
milk 14–15
mothers 11–12, 14–18